COUNTRY LIVING
collection

Diary 2024

Personal details

Name
_____

Address
_____

_____

_____

_____

Telephone (home)
_____

Telephone (work)
_____

Telephone (mobile)
_____

Fax
_____

E-mail
_____

● New Moon   ◖ First Quarter   ○ Full Moon   ◗ Last Quarter

2024 year planner

January
M	1	8	15	22	29
T	2	9	16	23	30
W	3	10	17	24	31
T	4	11	18	25	·
F	5	12	19	26	·
S	6	13	20	27	·
S	7	14	21	28	·

February
M	·	5	12	19	26
T	·	6	13	20	27
W	·	7	14	21	28
T	1	8	15	22	29
F	2	9	16	23	·
S	3	10	17	24	·
S	4	11	18	25	·

March
M	·	4	11	18	25
T	·	5	12	19	26
W	·	6	13	20	27
T	·	7	14	21	28
F	1	8	15	22	29
S	2	9	16	23	30
S	3	10	17	24	31

April
M	1	8	15	22	29
T	2	9	16	23	30
W	3	10	17	24	·
T	4	11	18	25	·
F	5	12	19	26	·
S	6	13	20	27	·
S	7	14	21	28	·

May
M	·	6	13	20	27
T	·	7	14	21	28
W	1	8	15	22	29
T	2	9	16	23	30
F	3	10	17	24	31
S	4	11	18	25	·
S	5	12	19	26	·

June
M	·	3	10	17	24
T	·	4	11	18	25
W	·	5	12	19	26
T	·	6	13	20	27
F	·	7	14	21	28
S	1	8	15	22	29
S	2	9	16	23	30

July
M	1	8	15	22	29
T	2	9	16	23	30
W	3	10	17	24	31
T	4	11	18	25	·
F	5	12	19	26	·
S	6	13	20	27	·
S	7	14	21	28	·

August
M	·	5	12	19	26
T	·	6	13	20	27
W	·	7	14	21	28
T	1	8	15	22	29
F	2	9	16	23	30
S	3	10	17	24	31
S	4	11	18	25	·

September
M	30	2	9	16	23
T	·	3	10	17	24
W	·	4	11	18	25
T	·	5	12	19	26
F	·	6	13	20	27
S	·	7	14	21	28
S	1	8	15	22	29

October
M	·	7	14	21	28
T	1	8	15	22	29
W	2	9	16	23	30
T	3	10	17	24	31
F	4	11	18	25	·
S	5	12	19	26	·
S	6	13	20	27	·

November
M	·	4	11	18	25
T	·	5	12	19	26
W	·	6	13	20	27
T	·	7	14	21	28
F	1	8	15	22	29
S	2	9	16	23	30
S	3	10	17	24	·

December
M	30	2	9	16	23
T	31	3	10	17	24
W	·	4	11	18	25
T	·	5	12	19	26
F	·	6	13	20	27
S	·	7	14	21	28
S	1	8	15	22	29

2025 year planner

January
M	·	6	13	20	27
T	·	7	14	21	28
W	1	8	15	22	29
T	2	9	16	23	30
F	3	10	17	24	31
S	4	11	18	25	·
S	5	12	19	26	·

February
M	·	3	10	17	24
T	·	4	11	18	25
W	·	5	12	19	26
T	·	6	13	20	27
F	·	7	14	21	28
S	1	8	15	22	·
S	2	9	16	23	·

March
M	31	3	10	17	24
T	·	4	11	18	25
W	·	5	12	19	26
T	·	6	13	20	27
F	·	7	14	21	28
S	1	8	15	22	29
S	2	9	16	23	30

April
M	·	7	14	21	28
T	1	8	15	22	29
W	2	9	16	23	30
T	3	10	17	24	·
F	4	11	18	25	·
S	5	12	19	26	·
S	6	13	20	27	·

May
M	·	5	12	19	26
T	·	6	13	20	27
W	·	7	14	21	28
T	1	8	15	22	29
F	2	9	16	23	30
S	3	10	17	24	31
S	4	11	18	25	·

June
M	30	2	9	16	23
T	·	3	10	17	24
W	·	4	11	18	25
T	·	5	12	19	26
F	·	6	13	20	27
S	·	7	14	21	28
S	1	8	15	22	29

July
M	·	7	14	21	28
T	1	8	15	22	29
W	2	9	16	23	30
T	3	10	17	24	31
F	4	11	18	25	·
S	5	12	19	26	·
S	6	13	20	27	·

August
M	·	4	11	18	25
T	·	5	12	19	26
W	·	6	13	20	27
T	·	7	14	21	28
F	1	8	15	22	29
S	2	9	16	23	30
S	3	10	17	24	31

September
M	1	8	15	22	29
T	2	9	16	23	30
W	3	10	17	24	·
T	4	11	18	25	·
F	5	12	19	26	·
S	6	13	20	27	·
S	7	14	21	28	·

October
M	·	6	13	20	27
T	·	7	14	21	28
W	1	8	15	22	29
T	2	9	16	23	30
F	3	10	17	24	31
S	4	11	18	25	·
S	5	12	19	26	·

November
M	·	3	10	17	24
T	·	4	11	18	25
W	·	5	12	19	26
T	·	6	13	20	27
F	·	7	14	21	28
S	1	8	15	22	29
S	2	9	16	23	30

December
M	1	8	15	22	29
T	2	9	16	23	30
W	3	10	17	24	31
T	4	11	18	25	·
F	5	12	19	26	·
S	6	13	20	27	·
S	7	14	21	28	·

Welcome

Thank you for choosing this *Country Living* diary to record all your important events throughout the year. The ebb and flow of the seasons is such an important part of British life and our countryside, and every stunning portrait in this diary has been chosen to reflect that and inspire you. The images have all appeared in our monthly magazines and are the cream of a very superior crop! We hope you love our selection as much as we do. Enjoy!

Louise Pearce

Editor-in-chief
Country Living Magazine

PS For more details of the world of *Country Living* and our events throughout the year, visit *countryliving.com/uk*

January

1
Monday

New Year's Day (Holiday UK, R. of Ireland, USA, CAN, AUS, NZL)

2
Tuesday

Holiday (SCT, NZL)

3
Wednesday

4
Thursday

5
Friday

6
Saturday

7
Sunday

8

Monday

9

Tuesday

10

Wednesday

●

11

Thursday

12

Friday

13

Saturday

14

Sunday

Jules Hogan (knitwear) featured in *Country Living* January 2022

January

15
Monday

Martin Luther King, Jr. Day (Holiday USA)

16
Tuesday

17
Wednesday

18
Thursday

19
Friday

20
Saturday

21
Sunday

22
Monday

23
Tuesday

24
Wednesday

25
Thursday

○

Burns Night (SCT)

26
Friday

Australia Day (Holiday AUS)

27
Saturday

28
Sunday

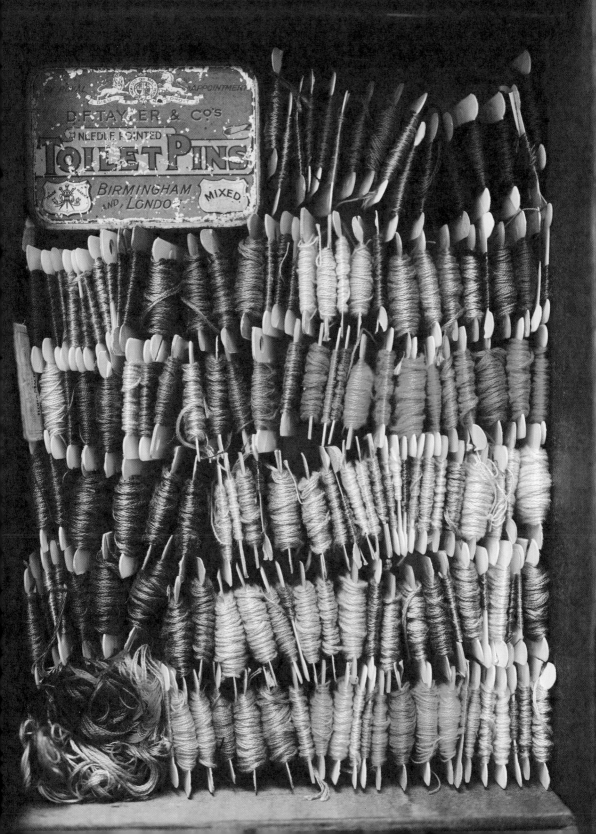

January/February

29
Monday

30
Tuesday

31
Wednesday

1
Thursday

☽

2
Friday

3
Saturday

4
Sunday

5
Monday   St Brigid's Day (Holiday R. of Ireland)

6
Tuesday   Waitangi Day (Holiday NZL)

7
Wednesday

8
Thursday

9
Friday

10
Saturday   Chinese New Year - Year of the Dragon

11
Sunday

February

12

Monday

13

Tuesday

Shrove Tuesday

14

Wednesday

St Valentine's Day / Ash Wednesday

15

Thursday

☽

16

Friday

17

Saturday

18

Sunday

19
Monday

Presidents' Day (Holiday USA)

20
Tuesday

21
Wednesday

22
Thursday

23
Friday

○

24
Saturday

25
Sunday

February / March

26

Monday

27

Tuesday

28

Wednesday

29

Thursday

1

Friday

St David's Day

2

Saturday

◐

3

Sunday

March

4
Monday

5
Tuesday

6
Wednesday

7
Thursday

8
Friday

9
Saturday

●

10
Sunday

Mothering Sunday (UK, R. of Ireland) / Ramadan Begins at Sundown

COUNTRY LIVING
collection

March

11
Monday

12
Tuesday

13
Wednesday

14
Thursday

15
Friday

16
Saturday

◑

17
Sunday

St Patrick's Day

COUNTRY LIVING
collection

18
Monday *Holiday (N. Ireland, R. of Ireland)*

19
Tuesday

20
Wednesday

21
Thursday

22
Friday

23
Saturday

24
Sunday

March

○

25
Monday

26
Tuesday

27
Wednesday

28
Thursday

29
Friday

Good Friday (Holiday UK, CAN, AUS, NZL)

30
Saturday

31
Sunday

Easter Sunday / British Summer Time begins

1
Monday

Easter Monday (Holiday UK except SCT, R. of Ireland, CAN, AUS, NZL)

◑

2
Tuesday

3
Wednesday

4
Thursday

5
Friday

6
Saturday

7
Sunday

April

●

8
Monday

9
Tuesday

Eid al-Fitr Begins at Sundown

10
Wednesday

11
Thursday

12
Friday

13
Saturday

14
Sunday

15
Monday

16
Tuesday

17
Wednesday

18
Thursday

19
Friday

20
Saturday

21
Sunday

April

22
Monday

Passover Begins at Sundown

23
Tuesday

St George's Day

○

24
Wednesday

25
Thursday

Anzac Day (Holiday AUS, NZL)

26
Friday

27
Saturday

28
Sunday

29
Monday

30
Tuesday

Passover Ends at Sundown

1
Wednesday

◐

2
Thursday

3
Friday

4
Saturday

5
Sunday

May

6

Monday

Holiday (UK, R. of Ireland)

7

Tuesday

●

8

Wednesday

9

Thursday

10

Friday

11

Saturday

12

Sunday

Mother's Day (USA, CAN, AUS, NZL)

13
Monday

14
Tuesday

15
Wednesday

16
Thursday

17
Friday

18
Saturday

19
Sunday

May

20
Monday

Victoria Day (Holiday CAN)

21
Tuesday

22
Wednesday

○

23
Thursday

24
Friday

25
Satur...

26
Sunday

27
Monday   *Holiday (UK) / Memorial Day (Holiday USA)*

28
Tuesday

29
Wednesday

30
Thursday

31
Friday

1
Saturday

2
Sunday

June

3
Monday

Holiday (R. of Ireland) / King's Birthday (Holiday NZL)

4
Tuesday

5
Wednesday

6
Thursday

7
Friday

8
Saturday

9
Sunday

10
Monday

11
Tuesday

12
Wednesday

13
Thursday

14
Friday

15
Saturday

16
Sunday

Father's Day (UK, R. of Ireland, USA, CAN)

June

17
Monday

18
Tuesday

19
Wednesday

Juneteenth (Holiday USA)

20
Thursday

21
Friday

○

22
Saturday

23
Sunday

24
Monday

25
Tuesday

26
Wednesday

27
Thursday

28
Friday

29
Saturday

30
Sunday

July

1
Monday

Canada Day (Holiday CAN)

2
Tuesday

3
Wednesday

4
Thursday

Independence Day (Holiday USA)

●

5
Friday

6
Saturday

7
Sunday

8
Monday

9
Tuesday

10
Wednesday

11
Thursday

12
Friday   *Battle of the Boyne (Holiday N. Ireland)*

◐

13
Saturday

14
Sunday

July

15
Monday

16
Tuesday

17
Wednesday

18
Thursday

19
Friday

20
Saturday

○

21
Sunday

22
Monday

23
Tuesday

24
Wednesday

25
Thursday

26
Friday

27
Saturday

28
Sunday

COUNTRY LIVING
collection

July / August

29
Monday

30
Tuesday

31
Wednesday

1
Thursday

2
Friday

3
Saturday

4
Sunday

5
Monday

Holiday (SCT, R. of Ireland)

6
Tuesday

7
Wednesday

8
Thursday

9
Friday

10
Saturday

11
Sunday

August

12
Monday

13
Tuesday

14
Wednesday

15
Thursday

16
Friday

17
Saturday

18
Sunday

○

19
Monday

20
Tuesday

21
Wednesday

22
Thursday

23
Friday

24
Saturday

25
Sunday

August / September

26
Monday

Holiday (UK except SCT)

27
Tuesday

28
Wednesday

29
Thursday

30
Friday

31
Saturday

1
Sunday

Father's Day (AUS, NZL)

2
Monday

Labor Day (Holiday USA) / Labour Day (Holiday CAN)

3
Tuesday

●

4
Wednesday

5
Thursday

6
Friday

7
Saturday

8
Sunday

September

9
Monday

10
Tuesday

◑

11
Wednesday

12
Thursday

13
Friday

14
Saturday

15
Sunday

16
Monday

17
Tuesday

○

18
Wednesday

19
Thursday

20
Friday

21
Saturday

22
Sunday

Nicola Hornsby from Achray Farm featured in *Country Living* September 2022

September

23
Monday

24
Tuesday

25
Wednesday

26
Thursday

27
Friday

28
Saturday

29
Sunday

COUNTRY LIVING
collection

30
Monday

1
Tuesday

2
Wednesday

●

3
Thursday

4
Friday

5
Saturday

6
Sunday

October

7

Monday

8

Tuesday

9

Wednesday

◑

10

Thursday

11

Friday

12

Saturday

13

Sunday

COUNTRY LIVING

collection

14
Monday

Columbus Day (Holiday USA) / Thanksgiving Day (Holiday CAN)

15
Tuesday

16
Wednesday

17
Thursday

18
Friday

19
Saturday

20
Sunday

The Honourable
One of the Justices of her Maj[?]
and Recorder of the

October

21
Monday

22
Tuesday

23
Wednesday

24
Thursday

25
Friday

26
Saturday

27
Sunday

British Summer Time ends

28
Monday

Holiday (R. of Ireland) / Labour Day (Holiday NZL)

29
Tuesday

30
Wednesday

31
Thursday

Hallowe'en

1
Friday

●

Diwali

2
Saturday

3
Sunday

November

4

Monday

5

Tuesday

Bonfire Night

6

Wednesday

7

Thursday

8

Friday

◑

9

Saturday

10

Sunday

Remembrance Sunday (UK)

COUNTRY LIVING
collection

11
Monday

Veterans Day (Holiday USA) / Remembrance Day (Holiday CAN)

12
Tuesday

13
Wednesday

14
Thursday

○

15
Friday

16
Saturday

17
Sunday

November

18
Monday

19
Tuesday

20
Wednesday

21
Thursday

22
Friday

◐

23
Saturday

24
Sunday

25
Monday

26
Tuesday

27
Wednesday

28
Thursday

Thanksgiving Day (Holiday USA)

29
Friday

30
Saturday

St Andrew's Day

●

1
Sunday

December

2

Monday

Holiday (SCT)

3

Tuesday

4

Wednesday

5

Thursday

6

Friday

7

Saturday

◑

8

Sunday

9
Monday

10
Tuesday

11
Wednesday

12
Thursday

13
Friday

14
Saturday

○

15
Sunday

Neary Nogs Chocolate featured in *Country Living* December 2022

December

16
Monday

17
Tuesday

18
Wednesday

19
Thursday

20
Friday

21
Saturday

22
Sunday

23
Monday

24
Tuesday

Christmas Eve

25
Wednesday

Christmas Day (Holiday UK, R. of Ireland, USA, CAN, AUS, NZL)

26
Thursday

Boxing Day, St Stephen's Day (Holiday UK, R. of Ireland, CAN, AUS, NZL)

27
Friday

28
Saturday

29
Sunday

December / January 2025

30

Monday

31

New Year's Eve

Tuesday

1

New Year's Day (Holiday UK, R. of Ireland, USA, CAN, AUS, NZL)

Wednesday

2

Holiday (SCT, NZL)

Thursday

3

Friday

4

Saturday

5

Sunday

Addresses

Name

Address

E-mail

Telephone   Mobile

Name

Address

E-mail

Telephone   Mobile

Name

Address

E-mail

Telephone   Mobile

Name

Address

E-mail

Telephone   Mobile

Name

Address

E-mail

Telephone   Mobile

Addresses

Name

Address

E-mail

Telephone   Mobile

Name

Address

E-mail

Telephone   Mobile

Name

Address

E-mail

Telephone   Mobile

Name

Address

E-mail

Telephone   Mobile

Name

Address

E-mail

Telephone   Mobile

Addresses

Name

Address

E-mail

Telephone   Mobile

Name

Address

E-mail

Telephone   Mobile

Name

Address

E-mail

Telephone   Mobile

Name

Address

E-mail

Telephone   Mobile

Name

Address

E-mail

Telephone   Mobile

Addresses

Name

Address

E-mail

Telephone   Mobile

Name

Address

E-mail

Telephone   Mobile

Name

Address

E-mail

Telephone   Mobile

Name

Address

E-mail

Telephone   Mobile

Name

Address

E-mail

Telephone   Mobile

Addresses

Name

Address

E-mail

Telephone   Mobile

Name

Address

E-mail

Telephone   Mobile

Name

Address

E-mail

Telephone   Mobile

Name

Address

E-mail

Telephone   Mobile

Name

Address

E-mail

Telephone   Mobile

Addresses

Name

Address

E-mail

Telephone   Mobile

Name

Address

E-mail

Telephone   Mobile

Name

Address

E-mail

Telephone   Mobile

Name

Address

E-mail

Telephone   Mobile

Name

Address

E-mail

Telephone   Mobile

Addresses

Name

Address

E-mail

Telephone   Mobile

Name

Address

E-mail

Telephone   Mobile

Name

Address

E-mail

Telephone   Mobile

Name

Address

E-mail

Telephone   Mobile

Name

Address

E-mail

Telephone   Mobile

Addresses

Name

Address

E-mail

Telephone   Mobile

Name

Address

E-mail

Telephone   Mobile

Name

Address

E-mail

Telephone   Mobile

Name

Address

E-mail

Telephone   Mobile

Name

Address

E-mail

Telephone   Mobile

Notes

Notes

Notes

Notes

Notes

Notes

Notes

Notes

Notes

Notes

Notes